MAKING ORIGINAL & PORTRAIT DOLLS
IN CERNIT

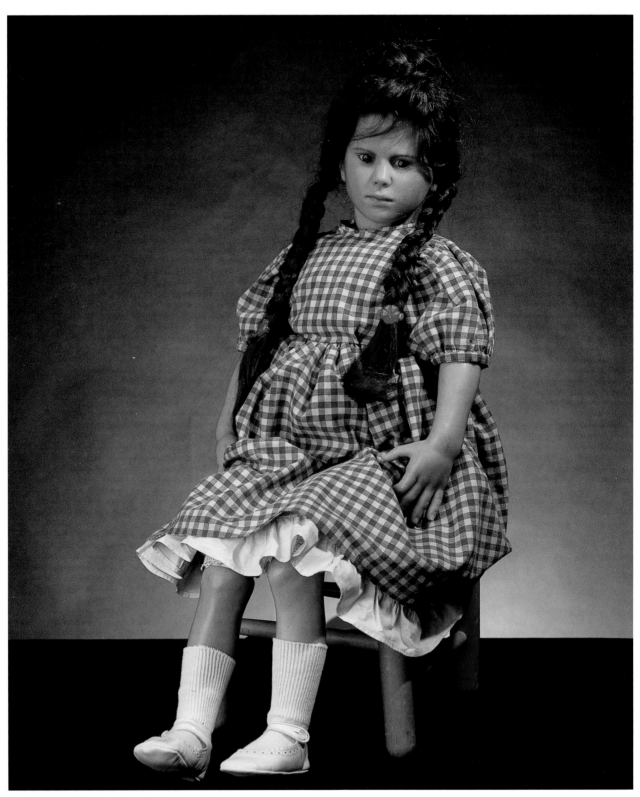

The *original Rotraut Doll*, Cernit, 33in (84cm), made by the author in 1990 after her own childhood photograph.
Right page: Rotraut Schrott - a current photographic study.

Rotraut Schrott

MAKING ORIGINAL
&
PORTRAIT DOLLS IN CERNIT

Illustration above: *Gabriela*, 34in (86cm), 1988.
Illustrations left page above: *Felicity*, 33in (84cm), 1990 and *Elke* (portrait), 33in (84cm), 1991; below: Noreen, 34in (86cm), 1989.

Concept and Layout: Joachim F. Richter
Text and Captions:
Christian Hufnagel, Rotraut Schrott, Georg Schrott, Ludwig Adam, Joachim F. Richter.
Photographs: Georg Schrott, Joachim F. Richter, Studio AIM, Sabine Schürfeld, GADCO.
Anatomy studies: Ludwig Adam.
Translation: Michael Robertson.
© 1991 by Verlag Laterna magica
     Joachim F. Richter, München,
     Federal Republic of Germany.
ISBN: 0-87588-394-X
Printed in Germany.

From my father, a passionate artist, came my artistic talent, which was surely placed in my cradle by him.

Table of Contents

Acknowledgements

My father, Ludwig Adams, is the key behind my artistic talent. As a child, I admired his ability to take his palette and brushes and create beautiful landscapes. What especially attracted my attention was his ability to make abstract images appear alive on canvas. To him I would like to offer a special thanks for his advice, guidance and most importantly for teaching me to strive for perfectionism in my artistic ventures.

A very special thanks also to my husband who, despite his busy professional life, has found patience with my doll making activities. I would also like to thank him for photographing all the dolls you see in this book as well as helping me with the written text. Without him this book would not have been possible.

Rotraut Schrott

Rotraut Schrott

Introduction

The high level of success, representing the works of great doll makers, has caused the triumphal advance of the artist doll. These creations provide important cultural contemporary doll art. They have attained a most beloved place in our hearts and in the doll world that the price does not play so important a role in our decision to possess one. It is the beauty that captures our eyes and hearts not the value or price.

One of the most artistically gifted artists of the international doll world is Rotraut Schrott, who knows how to fascinate a demanding public. Her works of art convey not only independence and unmistakability, but a diversity not to be surpassed by the characters and types. These are extraordinary portrait dolls which emerge under her expert hands from child models or photographs as well as fairy tale or historically oriented creations. Whether it be Little Red Riding Hood, Cinderella or the music playing Mozart, Rotraut Schrott has the rare ability to present these figures more optimally in their perfection, through fantasiful design and handmade clothes.

Thus nothing would bring more honor than to dedicate this exquisite book to such an intriguing doll artist who has inspired the whole world with her realistic life work of art. With the publication of this book Rotraut Schrott's artistic creations are captured forever, exemplifying her as a model for the new generation of doll makers. The inquisitive public will find a genuine work book with valuable hints on how to create your own doll masterpieces.

Joachim F. Richter

Joachim F. Richter, Publisher

About the doll artist Rotraut Schrott

Illustration above: *Jonnie*, 34-1/8in (87cm), 1990.

Illustration left page: *Jonnie and Jennie*, 34-1/8in (87cm) and 33in (84cm), 1990.

Self criticism has enabled me to improve my works of art constantly.

Rotraut Schrott

These faces cannot lie. They are the countenance of human perception. In their expression all pain and joy of this world are found, the tears of solitude, the calm pouting lips of despair, the eye winking of larcenous delight, the large pupils of curiosity, the turning of the whispers of innocence and the radiating smile of those being loved.

For the wildly curled Katalin, the disheveled Lukas or the angel Martina time will not hurt their innocence. Although these boys and girls share an unusual fate, they are children and will remain so always, no blood will flow in their bodies, no heart will beat in their chest. These children are not from this world. They are dolls and at the same time are not.

The creations of Rotraut Schrott are different from other dolls because of the material from which they are formed. The face, chest, arms and legs are made from a resin-type mass (Cernit), the bodies from cotton wool. Only those who take these children into their arms can perceive the coldness, a disappointment, which many have already learned. The small favorites seduce us to touch them. They own a certain characteristic, one that places them far over the status of a doll: a similarity to their human counterparts missing the dolliness of their brothers and sisters in the toy industry.

This feature alone has won recognition for Rotraut's work, but the mother of three grown up children has not stopped at this level but continued to the next, capturing a likeness of the human appearance in the creation of her dolls. In order to capture this human spirit, the doll must be sculpted to perfection expelling everything unnaturally symmetrical and uniform from these faces and incorporating into each doll an unmistakable character in the literal sense. Even though the red curled Marlene and Martina with the long brown hair may be of the same age, worlds separate these two doll-girls. An expectation of being a woman surrounds Marlene, announced by the two narrow folds under the eyelids and the knowing, mocking lines around the mouth. From Martina's dark brown eyes and immaculately smooth face still speaks the soul of a dreamy and romantic girl, which surely knows itself still to be in the lap of security as a child.

Illustration on left page and above: Portrait baby with head band, 25in (64cm), 1991.

Illustration above: *Baby Fritzi*, 24-1/2in (62cm), 1987.

With the ability to create life from dead material, Rotraut Schrott brings a new dimension into the arts and crafts of a communicated guild. With her, the doll maker becomes the artist. Because there are countless definitions of art, it is indisputable whether an object with its own reality and mystery can be formed from deformed mass. Much can be explained, can be imitated from nature, can be learned; but that selfness each doll personifies can only be explained by Rotraut Schrott. "It often happens, that visitors talk to my dolls, because they believe them to be alive." Such a misfortune can be taken as a compliment and confirmation of her excellent work. How is it possible for her to give dolls this magnetism; remains an unanswered question because it cannot be answered with words but with talent.

Rotraut Schrott breaks open the picture of dolls, making them not only cute playing comrades or cool decoys for modeling current fashions but works of art. Each doll is an original since Rotraut refuses to use the technology of a cast for the original because then a doll could be copied in porcelain. Thus, these artist dolls emerge as originals, signed, and furnished with a certificate of authenticity.

The success and position Rotraut Schrott's "children" hold in the doll market shows itself within two phenomena. Like pictures and sculptures, her artist dolls are also collected as collectors' pieces and as objects of value, bought and sought after by museums and galleries all around the world. As the graphic artist duplicates his ideas set into a picture so that a broader public can be reached, such is the same with some of the creations produced in the metropolitan suburb of Baldham. These creations are manufactured in America in series and produced in either vinyl as a robust doll toy, or in porcelain as a jewel to be displayed in the home.

This international success distinguishes Rotraut Schrott as a cultural ambassador, but the choice of her motives already grants her this title. It is always the children that stand as models for the artist, not only as an idea in spirit but as a portrait. The spectrum of faces stretches around the whole world. Each nationality and temperament — from Europe to Asia to Africa — is represented. Priority by choice is artistic interest, because compared with an adult's face, it is far more difficult to model the face of a child. The viewer perceives far deeper love, as the artist expresses the characteristics of childhood. "I love their irrationality and spontaneity," exclaims Rotraut Schrott over the supposedly small and weak of our society. The adult world with all its

Illustration above and on left page: *Lisa*, 33in (84cm), 1990.

Tatjana with braids, 32-1/4in (82cm), 1985.

reason rarely sees the real characteristics of the child which may be disadvantageous to them, so that the very old saying can be seen: Children hold the mirror in front of themselves. Rotraut Schrott's dolls make us touch them and seduce our hearts because of their ultimately lovable nature; appearing sensitive, shy, delicate, never reckless or moody, and look expectingly into the world.

Her great interest in children, which voluntarily inspires Rotraut Schrott's creativity, is exemplified in this poem by Rainer Maria Rilke:

Works of art are of endless solitude
and with nothing can so little be achieved as with criticism
Only love can hold and attain them
And can be quite just against them

The artist appears on her part to take to heart these four lines. She is intent in succeeding to model only "happy faces" with the soft lines of the old masters of painting like Rembrandt, Tizian or Leonardo da Vinci. For the public the warning from the poet appears to have an effect on the loving relationship between the visitors and the dolls.

Like many women who seek a career outside the home, Rotraut Schrott took art as a second educational career. Beginning in 1980, she took courses at the university level. In the course Doll Modeling Like In Grandmother's Time, she discovered her abilities and enthusiasm to model faces, but the craftmanship course alone did not satisfy her curiosity. "They were only little dolls, without ears, mouth and eyelashes," she exclaimed. However, the incentive was given. Rotraut worked both night and day to ensure that her first project was as close to perfection as it could possibly be. Her teacher was so enthralled by her work that she used Rotraut's technique as a guide for the other students. What seemed at the beginning to be a hobby, never became one, but instead developed immediately into a passion and a new feeling for life: "If I work on a face, I forget everything around me and feel completely relaxed."

Creativity accompanies Rotraut Schrott since her childhood. The artistic gift lies within the family. As a small girl, she watched her father work rather intensely, especially when he set-up his easel and started to conjure a beautiful landscape or a smile of a person on the canvas. She has inherited the talent to model naturally from her paternal guide, orienting her artist

Illustration above and on left page: *Ninotschka*, Russian, 33in (84cm), 1989. "I am 5-years old!"

Jonnie and Jennie on the slide, 34-1/4in (87cm) and 33in (84cm), 1990.

dolls very closely to the laws of the human anatomy. Even today, Rotraut continues to learn from her artist father, Ludwig Adam. The 78 year old Adams still likes to portray the people of his surroundings which explains the natural color talent Rotraut Schrott has gained. The eyes of her dolls are painted with transparent colors, the lips and cheeks receive a soft gleam by dabbing on Plaka colors. The finished doll has a natural tint and gleam in the eyes, which even the typical doll lacks because of the dull splendor of the glass eyes. Rotraut Schrott masters the art of painting the dolls as perfectly as her own sewing of the fantasiful clothes.

Meanwhile the family works together on doll production so that they can be admired two-dimensionally. While Adam produces a refreshing cheerful painted portrait of each original, her husband, Georg, photographs the dolls. His contribution is the one of reality since many people who look at the photos can see their children reflected in the dolls' actions.

After the course at the adult educational center, Rotraut has adjusted rather quickly to her success. The naturalness, the attractiveness and the expressional power of the artist dolls from the house of Schrott finds an enthusiastic echo within the doll world. Recommendations from collectors, press reports, exhibitions and prizes have provided Schrott with a renowned popularity in the doll making guild. At both of her first exhibitions, Christmas 1981 and 1982 in a large Munich department store, she attracted a large public. All of her exhibits were sold. One year later Rotraut received a first place prize from a company for doll parts in Frankfurt Main to distinguish her great artistic talent. After that exhibitions followed in Germany, France, Switzerland and America.

Growing popularity also has a price. Orders flutter into the house in such great numbers that participation in exhibitions has ended. "My dolls are never made independently, but always on order," says Schrott. Many parents of children long grown up place orders for plastic dolls to have a reproduction of those years. Until today the portrait dolls are the greatest challenge for Rotraut Schrott because each doll is an original, a separate idea that must have no connection to anything made before or after it. "I must always keep to the child's nature, that is the most difficult way to model." That she masters this task successfully is expressed by the confusion each client succumbs to. When the doll Nikoline sits at home on the living room chair, she must have such a convincing radiation of being alive that the grandmother with a joyful "Oh, there is my child" wants to take it into her

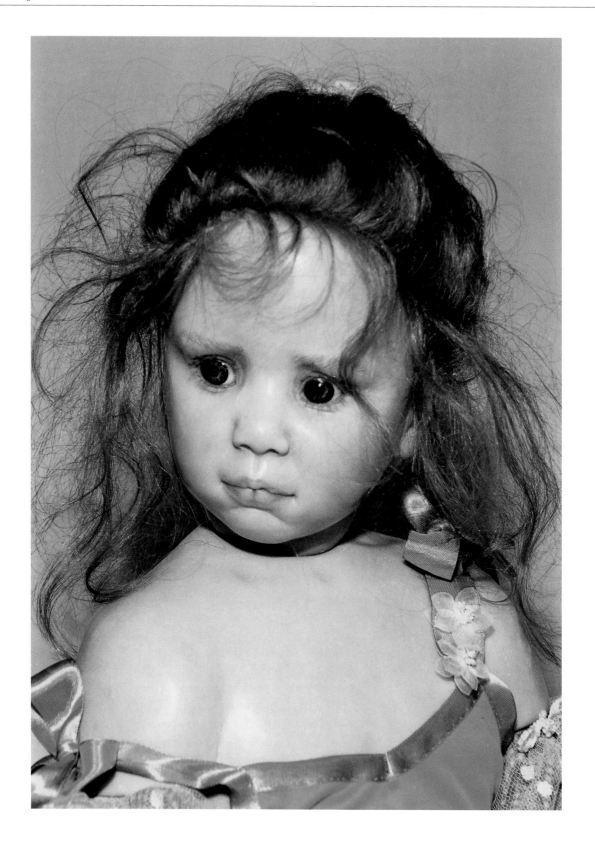

Illustration above and on left page: *Trixie*, small ballerina, 40in (100cm), 1989.

Lothar sitting, 33in (84cm), 1989.

arms. Only in the second moment does it dawn on the grandmother that Nikoline is only a doll and that the granddaughter has long since outgrown her childish shoes.

Although her creations appeared in Germany in 1985 for the first time in an artist doll book, the triumphal procession of her children actually began in America. The Schrott's were telephoned one evening by The Great American Doll Company (GADCO). The American public was so enthusiastic over the Red Riding Hood made by the hands of Rotraut Schrott that GADCO wanted to bring a series of dolls into the market.

In the country of unlimited possibilities, Martina was the first one to make a career. The brown eyed girl rose to stardom. "Oh Martina, how mysteriously, exciting and serious you look. The feelings expressed in your eyes could fill a book," a glowing admirer composed. A trade magazine even distinguished this graceful nature with an award, being the most perfect model of her class. This doll magazine awarded the prize "Winner Doll's Award of Excellence" to Rotraut Schrott. A success which moved her to the foremost position within the international doll scene. The artist was also nominated in that same year by the IDA (International Doll Academy) in the class of "Doll Design Concept of the Year" as one of the five first-place winners. This award was for Martina made in bisque. The "Award of Excellence" was accepted by Rotraut Schrott during a 14 day promotion tour between New York and Alabama.

Martina was the first in a group of five dolls brought out on the market by GADCO under the title "Childrens' souls are fragile" in vinyl and in a limited edition bisque. The enthusiasm in the United States was so great, that a Rotraut Schrott fan club was founded. Two new creations produced in the doll room at Baldham are now conquering the hearts of Americans, the dark haired Jasmine and the red haired Trixie, "The Stars of the Children's Ballet." After a period of waiting, the Rotraut Schrott children are now appearing in German doll and toy shops.

Her success has not made Rotraut Schrott arrogant. Naturally it pleases her that her second children are finding so many adoptive parents, and naturally a certain amount of pride encompasses her when she happens to discuss a review of the past years and sketches her climbing success from the adult educational center to a "World-Class Artist" (GADCO). But she would not be an artist if she did not keep her goals in mind. Her name and fame do not hold the most importance to her; Rotraut hopes that Martina is a treasure to the public, not only because she is a

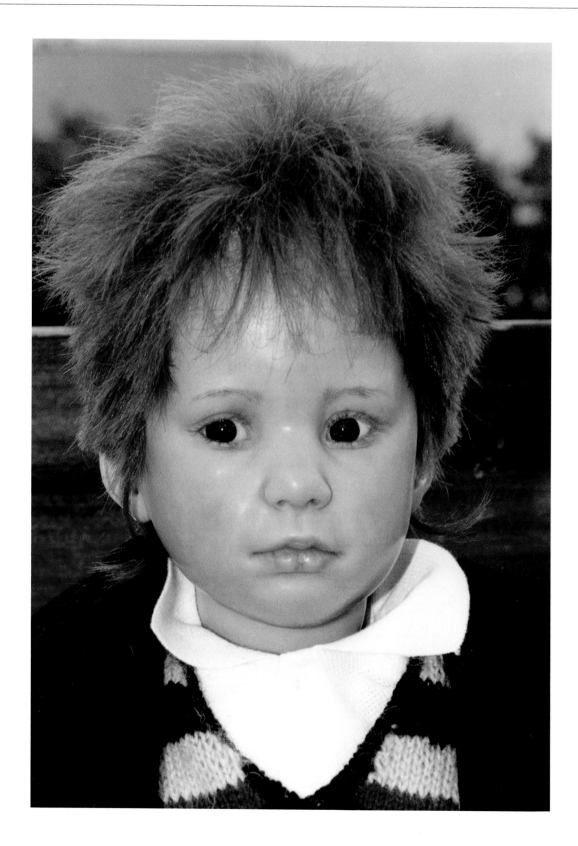

"Schrott Doll" but because she is an example of an innovative concept. Her artist dolls would rather "speak for themselves personally." She hopes that future creations made from such materials will not be of a different characteristic, but will personify the earnestness of the artist. Still no doll has been perfect. Each new face which awaits her is only one step in the endless, narrowing path of the ideal, perfection. Schrott wants to place her whole knowledge into this goal. The public will have to be patient to see which charming creations will leave from her workshop into the world and become "disappointments" to some since they are not alive.

Christian Hufnagel

Illustration left and on left page: *Lukas*, 34in (86cm), 1990.

Illustration below: *Svenja and Florian*, brother and sister, both 24-1/2in (88cm), 1988.

Jonnie, Marion and *Lukas* waiting for a train. 34-1/4in (87cm), 33in (84cm) and 34in (86cm), 1990.

If a doll is to look realistic, then her eyes must be able to speak. Therefore, I dedicate much of my time and love to this extremely important detail.

I do not know whether I could model villains; I would have to try! I strive to make my dolls radiate charm and security, sometimes even reflect a certain person.

Illustration on the right: *Monika* on a tricycle, "Look Mom! No hands!" 31-1/2in (80cm), 1991.

Body Proportions in Developing Humans

The One Year Old: The head is quite large (about a quarter of the body size) and sits on a short neck. The large trunk and chest stand out quite a bit with the large, round stomach arching forward. The navel lies somewhat below the center of the body. The arms and legs are bent and are shorter than the trunk in length.

The Two Year Old: The center of the body now lies around the navel area. The head with the trunk is about three head sizes, the legs two head sizes. The arms extend down to the top part of the thigh. In comparison to the upper part of the body, the arms and legs are short. The head is a fifth of the body size.

The Seven Year Old: The center of the body lies below the navel area. The legs and arms have become somewhat longer. The head is about a sixth of the total body size.

The Adult: The head and trunk form about half of the size of the body, the head about an eighth of the total size. The arms extend down about halfway on the thigh.

1-year-old
2-year-old
7-year-old
Mature
4 HL
5 HL
6 HL
8 HL
1 HL = 1 Head Length

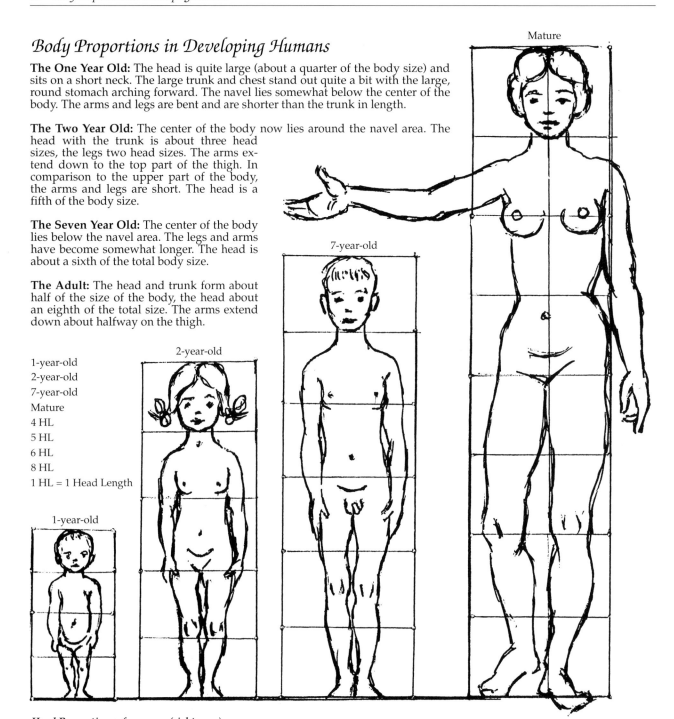

1-year-old

2-year-old

7-year-old

Mature

Head Proportions of a person (right page)

The One Year Old: The baby skull extends in profile from the front up to about a half of the head length of an adult. While on an adult the middle of the head length is equal to the eye axis, on a one and a six year old, the eye axis lies below the middle of the head length. Babies are still toothless. That is why the line of the mouth lies in the middle of the jaw partition.

The Six Year Old: Because the six year old is in the process of get-

ting new teeth, the lower jaw is somewhat higher than the upper jaw. The line of the mouth does not lie in the middle, the chin is longer in shape than the upper lip.

Looking at the skulls of each age group from above shows that the ears start from the center line and that the skull is broadest behind the ears. The skull of the one year old extends to about half of the depth in diameter of the human skull.

Head Proportions of a person

Draft of an ideal child's head from Paul Richer

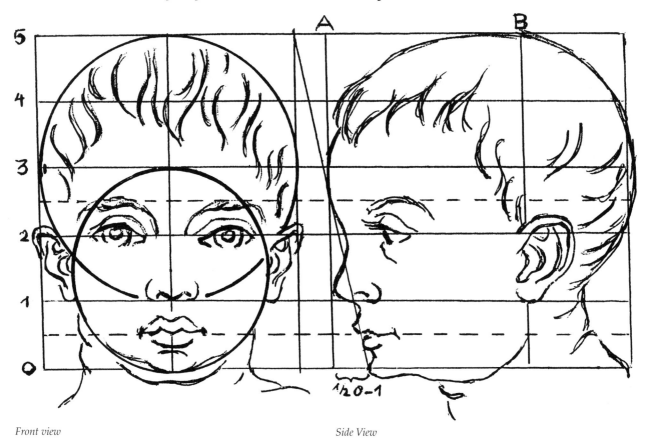

Front view   *Side View*

A straight vertical line is subdivided five times. Horizontal lines are drawn through these five division points. The width of the head is achieved by drawing a circle starting on line 3 with a 2 line radius. Then draw a vertical line through the center of the circle from 5 to 0. On this center line at the horizontal line 1.5, draw a circle with a raduius of 1.5. Now the proper shape of the view is given. The axis of the eyes lies on line 2, the outer edge of the eye angle lies on line 2, the inner eye angle lies slightly under line 2. The ears extend from about the upper eyelid down to line 1. The mouth axis lies in the middle between lines 0 to 1.

Identical scale with the front view. Next draw the outline of the front of the face starting at point A on line 5 and drawing outwards and down to line 1.

Curve the line inwards and continue to line 0. Mark half the distance between lines 0 and 1. Also mark the middle line between lines 2 and 3. These two points are then connected by a line which goes through the middle of line A. This slanting line indicates the location of the chin. The location of the eyes, nose and mouth is identical with that of the front view and similar with the location of the ear. The height of the skull (B) is gotten by taking the distance between 0 and 1, multiplying it by three and moving this distance upwards. The jaw bone ends at the connecting point between lines B and 1. This is also the starting point of the ear. From the top point of B the back of the head arches downward and stops shortly before the horizontal line 1 behind the ear; this is also the starting point of the throat.

Draft of an ideal adult's head from Paul Richer

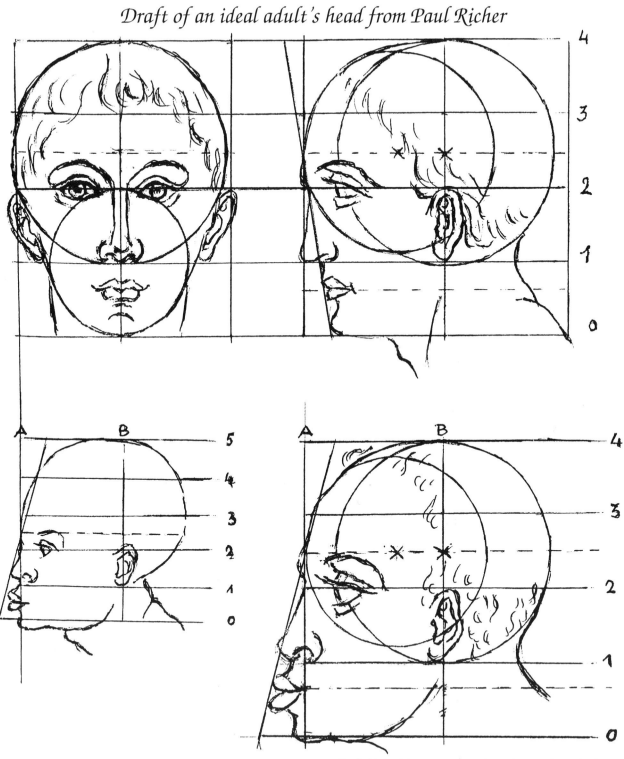

Profile of a black child.

Profile of a black adult; jaws projecting forwards, nostrils are clearly visible, very full lips.

The Mouth

The shape of the lips changes according to sex, age (the lips of children are red and swollen) and race. The ring muscle extends around both lips with the lip hump, delicate and soft, being an extension to the upper lip. The groove running down from the nose is called the Philtrum or love goblet, because it was seen by the Greeks as charming. With blacks one finds very full and protruding lips, because the jaw projects outwards.

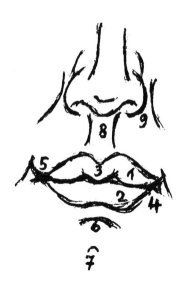

1. Upper lip
2. Lower lip
3. Hump
4. Corner of the Mouth
5. Corner nodules
6. Chin furrow
7. Chin dimples
8. Philtrum
   or
   Love goblet
9. Nose lip furrow

The Eye

The eyeball is the most important part of the eye. What is seen is only the part left free by the eyelids, which can be almond or slit shaped. The iris and pupil are surrounded by white sinew skin, which appears to be especially luminous with black skin color. In the middle of the eye the pupil and iris arch out as a transparent cornea. The iris gives the eye the color; blue, brown, green or gray in the shape of a ring. The pupil is a living diaphragm, now large or small according to the light needed. The eyelids are capable of widening the eye or narrowing them, whereby horizontal folds develop. With Asians the upper eyelid hangs far deeper in the inner eye corner, also called the Mongolian fold. The eyelids have at the edges delicate shapers, the eyelashes. On the lower eyelid one can especially see flashing of the iris, the watery surface of the eye. The expression on the face of a person is marked especially by the eyebrows over the eyes, because this defines the mental condition of the person.

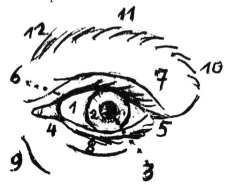

1. Sinew skin
2. Irises
3. Pupil
4. Corner of the inner eye
5. Corner of the outer eye
6. Upper eyelid
7. Upper eyelid fold
8. Lower eyelid
9. Cheek Fold
10. Eyebrow - Tail
11. Eyebrow - Body
12. Eyebrow - Head

The Ear

Ears of men are mostly larger and rougher than ears of women, which can be round, angular, standing out or flat.

In reference to the location of the ear one should point out that as a rule, the upper edge corresponds with the upper eyelid fold, the lower edge lies at the bottom edge of the nose. The auditory canal lies approximately on the same level of the upper edge of the nostrils. Accordingly, the ear-lobes lie between the lower edge of the nose and the upper edge of the nostrils.

Side view

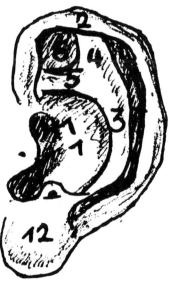

Front view

1. Auricle
2. Border edge
3. Opposite edge
4. Back branch
5. Front branch
6. Inner ear
7. Boat shaped furrow
8. Corner
9. Opposite corner
10. Lower and middle cut
11. Upper rounded Cut
12. Ear-lobe

Left arm and hand from the outside   *Right arm and hand from the inside*

The ell is found on the side of the pinky, the radius on the thumb side. Radius and ell are parallel if the palm is facing towards the front, the thumb towards the outside and the pinky towards the inside. In the illustration the thumb points towards the inside; therefore, the radius and ell are crossing each other.

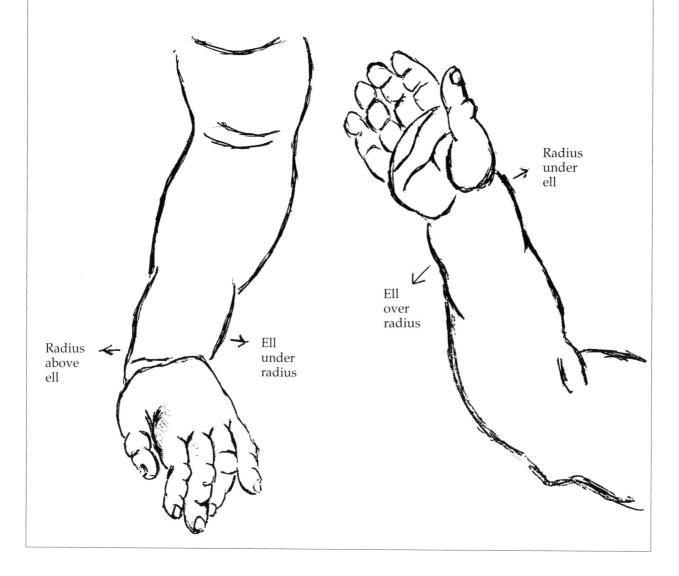

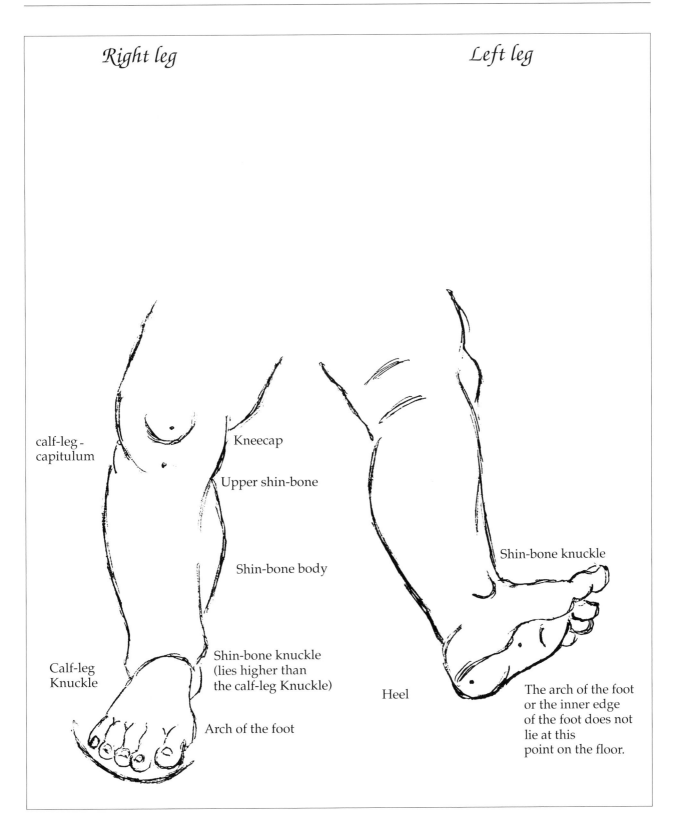

Right leg

Left leg

calf-leg-
capitulum

Kneecap

Upper shin-bone

Shin-bone body

Shin-bone knuckle

Calf-leg
Knuckle

Shin-bone knuckle
(lies higher than
the calf-leg Knuckle)

Heel

Arch of the foot

The arch of the foot
or the inner edge
of the foot does not
lie at this
point on the floor.

Tools, Modelling mass, colors

Rotraut Schrott:

Cernit as a Modelling Mass

The creation of sensitive doll faces as I would like to present allows for no concessions of reproductions and the use of molds; therefore, using Cernit provides space for the realization of such extreme expressions. This enables each doll to become a genuine original.

Cernit is a difficult material to handle compared to normal modelling clay, but if one learns to handle it then, it is impossible for them to use anything else. It is a material which radiates warmth, making the faces seem as if they are breathing the air of life.

My goal in this book is to pass on to the reader my experience with Cernit. This should and cannot be a classical modelling instruction book for the beginner, as has been published repeatedly, but a workbook of the concrete steps of portrait doll making. For me this is a difficult task, but nevertheless, it is one that holds the greatest importance in the doll making guild: being able to pass your own creativity to another. All of the experiences presented in the following work steps will not lead to the goal however, if the essentials are not taken into consideration:

- Get rid of the face characteristic to your work;

- Before you begin to model, study all the detail in the face to be portrayed:

a) Face form, e.g. round, oval, oblong, chubby, shape of the eyes round, oval, narrow, slanted...;

b) The shape of the triangle, which is determined by the distance between the eyes and the distance from the eyes to the mouth;

c) Length and shape of the nose, shape of the chin area, and finally of special significance the shape and expression of the mouth.

Fundamentally valid are, however, the body proportions for the respective age.

Since we will be dealing here with the doll Elke, a 5 year old girl, the following should be taken into consideration:

Total Size:	5 1/2 Head Lengths	(HL)
Torso length:	2	HL
Leg length:	2 1/2	HL
Arm length:	2 1/2-2 3/4	HL

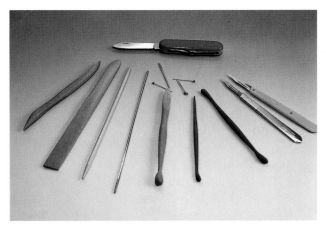

A picture of the modelling tools I use which may be considered unorthodox like knitting needles, pins and darners. The scalpel is a very important tool to use for cutting the excess Cernit away from the modelling mass. It is more useful than a knife because the scalpel is smaller in size allowing for greater mobility in small, delicate areas.

The modelling mass is transparent Cernit, which I mix with colored Cernit in brown, green, yellow and blue. The natural complexion of a European e.g. requires the kneading of 1kg (35.27oz) transparent Cernit with approximately 8g (.29oz) of brown Cernit.
Cernit - Green 1 ball of approx. 10mm (.39in) diameters
Cernit - Yellow 1 ball of approx. 10mm (.39in) diameters
Cernit - Blue 1 ball of approx. 10mm (.39in) diameters

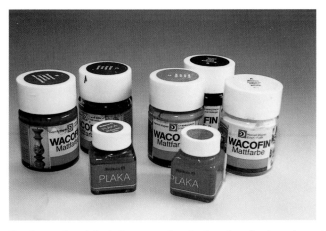

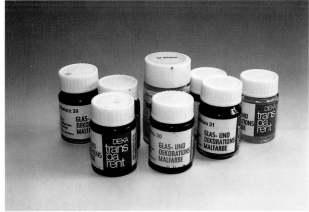

For the mouth and cheeks I use water-based paint colors, for the eyebrows Wacofin or Winsor & Newton artists acrylic colors or water-based paints. I paint the eyes with transparent Deka (fully transparent) oil based colors.

"My hands are my most important tool, although a scalpel, as well as knitting needles, pins and darners play an important role in my sculpting."

Elke, the model. ....

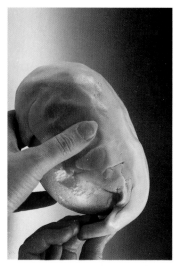

A solid Cernit dollhead would be too heavy for a doll, therefore I model it around a core of styrofoam (soft, pliable styrofoam). Halve a ball of styrofoam (diameter about 12cm [4.68in]) and cut this in half like the shape shown in the picture. European styrofoam has different properties than American styrofoam. Try using a ball of aluminium foil instead.

To not consume unnecessary amounts of Cernit modelling mass, add a piece of styrofoam to the halve ball at the side, which will become the forehead.

Now cover the core of styrofoam with enough Cernit modelling mass (so you are able to cut away excess), so that the area at the back of the head remains free, for better modelling purposes.

The ground shape of the head is already recognizable. I have considered that the child-model has a somewhat broader face.

Divide the front side of the head in 5 equal parts, using the tools as shown in this picture.

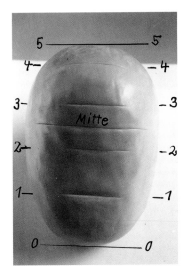

The lines are marked from 0 to 5 and the middle of the face is marked between 2 and 3.

On line (2) Mark the height of the eye with a suitable modeling wood (with spherical end). See Fig. on page 24.

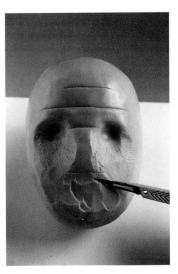

The underneath eye cavity material is now taken away with the scalpel. Whereby the forehead and nose appear, ...

... the final manufactured doll that appears in the following work steps.

... as a rule the nose of a child's face ends at the line (1).

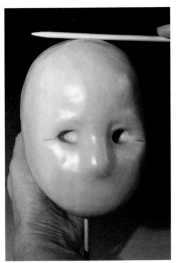

Now the real modeling begins. Try to give the forehead and eye cavities the right shape. It is especially important, to smooth the surface, a thick knitting needle will provide this.

In this picture one can clearly recognize the similarities of the eye cavities, the nose and the cheek area with the portrait photo. One can also see the small arch, the place at which the mouth will be worked at.

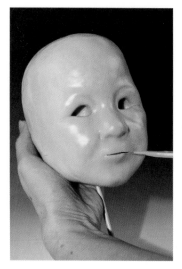

With a scalpel an incision is made in the mouth and opened to create room for the teeth.

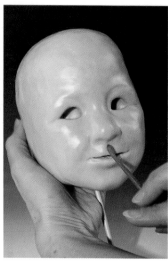

The nose furrow (Philtrum) is marked.

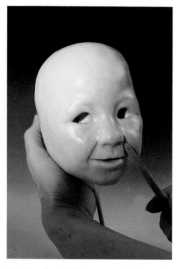

The laugh wrinkles are worked in with modelling wood.

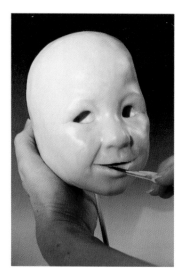

Now the mouth is opened further.

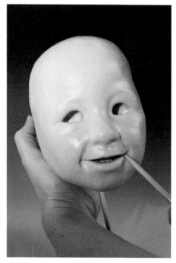

In this picture the length of the mouth is already determined, the corners of the mouth are marked and the oral cavity is made larger.

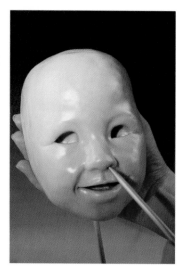

The smiling mouth of the girl is already modeled except for the teeth. Begin with the modeling of the nostrils, so as to give the nose its final shape.

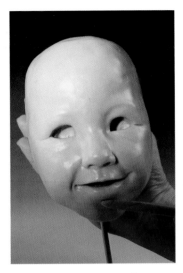

The chin receives its desired shape.

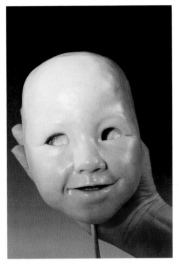

This picture shows the result of the current work.

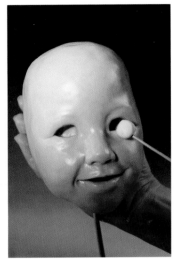

Using transparent Cernit, shape the eyeballs ...

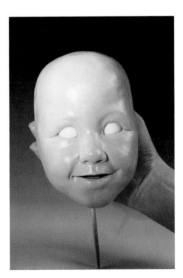

... and insert them into the eye cavities.

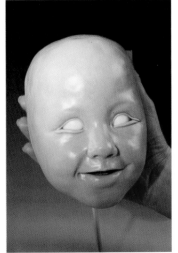

Place small rolled strips of modelling mass around the eyeballs. From these the upper and lower lids are created.

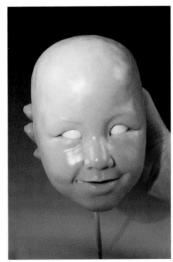

Make eye creases with a thin sewing needle.

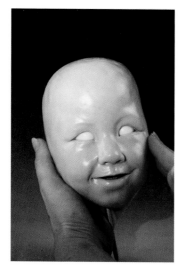

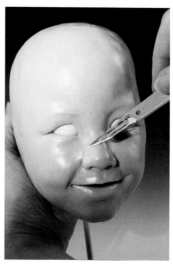

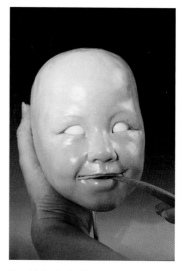

Unavoidable is the continuous remodeling of the already modelled parts, since Cernit tends to run.

My aim is to obtain the optimal identity of the doll with the child-model. Corrections may still be necessary in the advance stages, e.g. of the nose. Therefore, material should only be taken away, not added.

To add the teeth the jaw must be shaped. Again the base shape exists of two Cernit rolls, which are added to the oral cavity ...

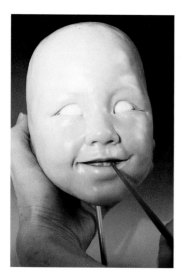

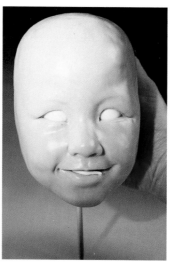

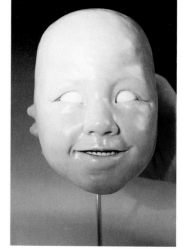

... and subsequently are shaped into the upper and lower jaw.

Now place a strip of transparent Cernit on the lower jaw and start to make the individual teeth. Although the lower teeth are hardly seen in the smiling mouth of the child, they are necessary for placing the upper teeth in the right order.

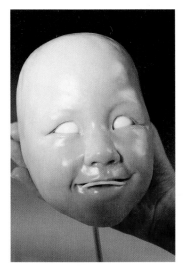

The same work occurs with the upper jaw.

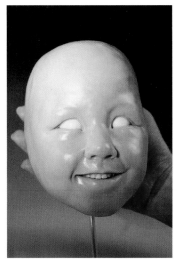

Since these teeth are fully visible, particular care is necessary when making these.

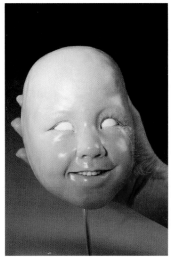

Between eyeball and eyelid scratch an incision with a needle and work in streaks for the eye lashes. Repeat the same thing for the lower eyelid. I use my own handmade real hair eyelashes.

It is far easier to produce the neck by itself and then finally attach it with the head. Shape a cylinder, penetrate it with a thick knitting needle. ...

... and continue working it, until the shape shown in the picture is visible.

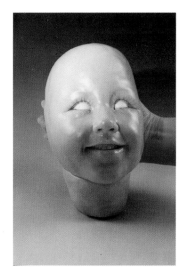

Finally the head is attached with the neck.

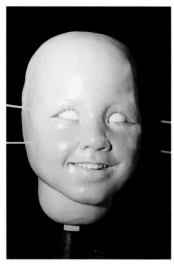

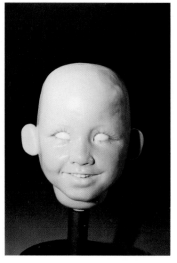

The basic shape for the ears is a 1.5cm (.59in) thick slice of Cernit.

The small wooden rods mark the location of the ears.

Half of the slice is now attached at the side to the head so that the ear extends from the upper eyelid fold down to the lower edge of the nose.

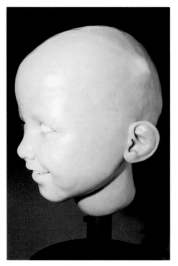

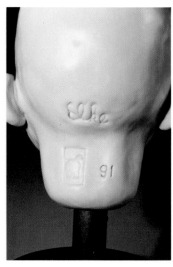

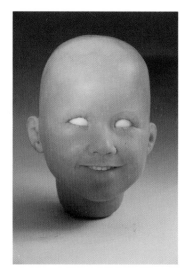

This picture shows the finished modeled ear. For further anatomy of the ear see page 27. Meanwhile I have also finished modeling the back of the head.

My trademark, the year and name of the child, seals the finished work.

This picture shows the hardened head after being in the oven for 60 minutes at 90°C (200°F).

For the production of the breast plate an auxiliary construction serves as a substructure. This substructure is covered with aluminum foil, so that the modelled breast plate can be easily taken off.

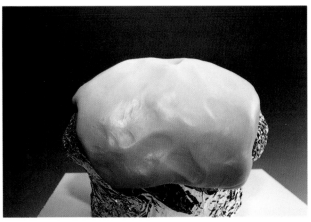

Now shape a 2cm (.78in) thick rectangular plate and place it over the substructure. The area, in which the neck is fitted into later, receives a small opening.

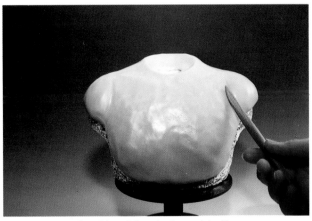

These two pictures show the way I shape the chest and shoulder area, ...

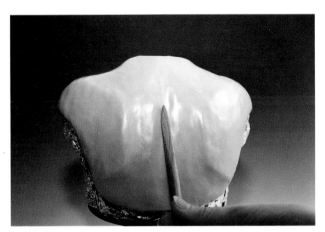

... the back area ...

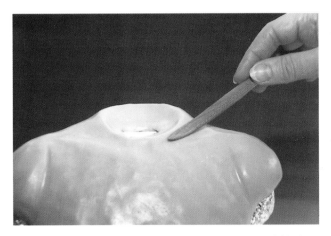

... and the throat area. I especially place large value on anatomical details like the working of the key bone, ...

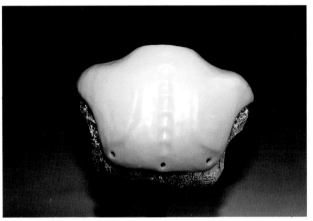

... spine and shoulder blades ...

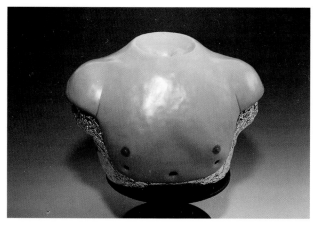

... and the lifelike dark colored Cernit nipples. Also, one can see three appropriate openings on the chest and on the back side which are required for attaching the head.

One can recognize from the side view of the breast plate that the throat section is not directly horizontal but goes down diagonally to the front.

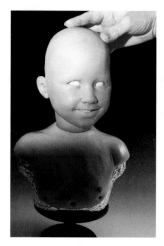

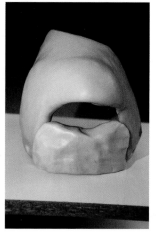

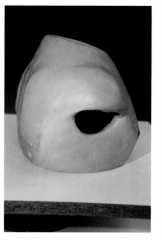

I get a close fit of neck and breast plate, whereby I compress the already fired head in the still soft breast plate.

The breast plate is now fired at 90°C (200°F) for 60 minutes, it is then removed from the substructure and the sides are then covered, and it is again fired at 90°C (200°F) degrees for 60 minutes. The sides can only be closed in a separate stage of work, since the closing of the chest below the shoulders would cause problems when removed from the mold.

This picture shows the finished breast plate with the head put on.

The devil lies in the detail! I say this because of all the time I have spent making the details like hands, toes, etcetera, more natural.

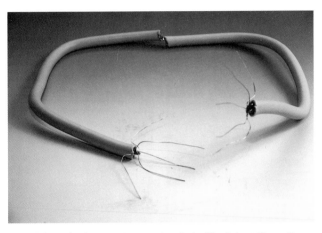

As a skeleton for the arms, I use an electrical cable of about 12mm diameter; a somewhat unusual process which has proven to work quite well. Instead of using the rather thick copper wires of the cable for the fingers, I use thin silver wire.

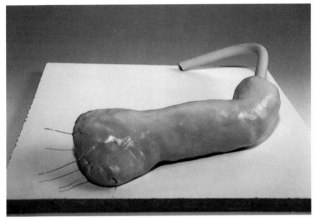

The skeleton is now surrounded with modelling mass ...

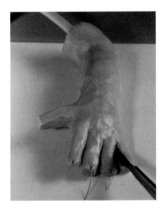

... and the arm and hand are worked out in a rough shape.

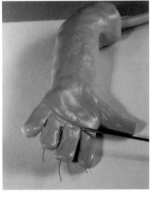

The starting points of the fingers are shown by drawing an arch from the index finger down to the small finger.

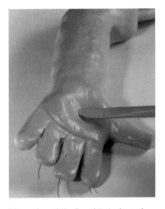

The palm of the hand is indented.

By scraping away material from the arm and fingers, the right shape is formed.

The ball of the hand is then modeled, the approximate finger length is determined.

A good guide for this is to use one's own hand as a guide.

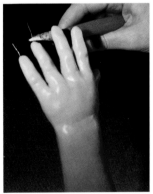

The remaining wire is cut away.

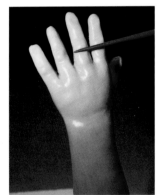

Do not forget to model the finger joints on the outside ...

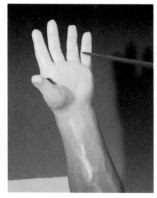

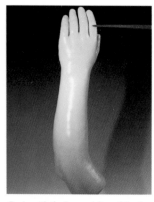

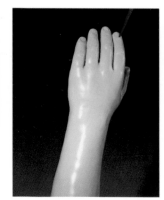

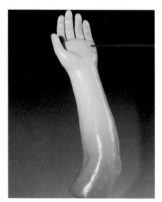

... and on the inside of the hand.

Begin with the fine modeling of the details, joint folds, ...

.... bed of the nails, ...

... the lines of the inner hand area and the working out of the arm.

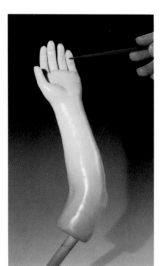

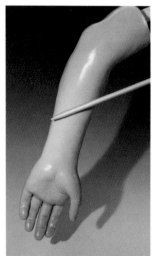

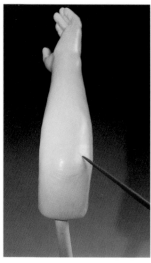

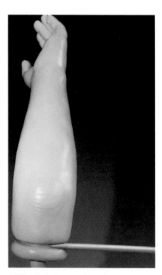

Important rule: Index and ring finger extend up to the middle of the last joint of the middle finger, the small finger up to the beginning of the last joint of the ring finger, the thumb extends barely to the end of the first joint of the index finger. Always remodel and smooth over and over again.

The folds of the crook of the elbow are incised.

With a knitting needle make a groove at the end of the arm, necessary for connecting the cloth upper arm to it.

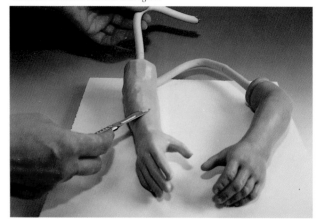

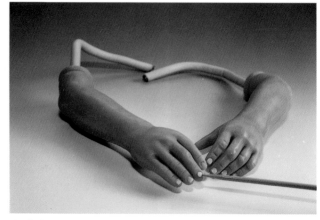

The finished arm serves as an important reference point for modeling the second arm.

On the finished and hardened arms and hands (at 90°C [200°F], 60 minutes) fingernails are modeled into the nail bed of the fingers; once again everything is fired.

As with the arms, I also use electrical cables as a skeleton for the legs. The exposed copper wiring also serves as a support for the foot.

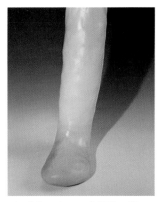

The skeleton is covered thickly with modelling mass.

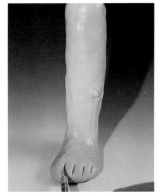

The toes are marked.

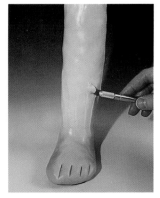

Begin to carve the shape of the lower legs.

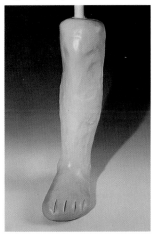

The shape of the lower legs is already well recognizable in the front ...

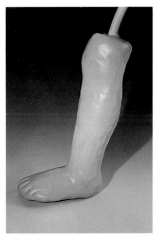

... and side view, the knee is indicated.

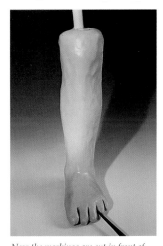

Now the markings are cut in front of the foot and the toes are modeled.

Again, the shape of the foot is made by taking away the excess material. The lower leg and knee are completely modelled, now smooth them out.

Finally come the details: nail beds and joint folds are worked out.

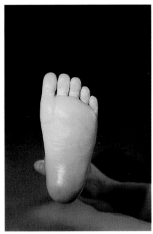

One should not forget to reproduce the sole of the foot as naturally as possible. (See page 29).

As with the arms, a groove is made above the knee for connecting.

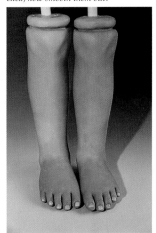

As with the hands, the toes of the previously hardened feet are also furnished with nails.

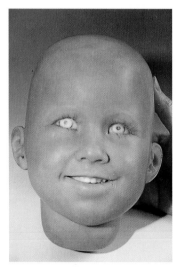

Drawn and painted eyes bring more warmth, expressional power and liveliness than glass eyes. With a pencil draw the iris and pupil and determine the direction of sight of the eye.

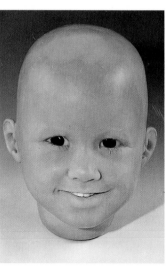

The iris is painted with the respective eye color. For this I use transparent Deka; in this case they are brown eyes.

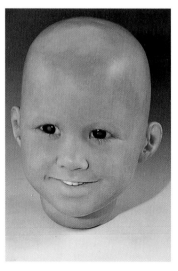

Finally the eye center is thinned with colorless Deka. ...

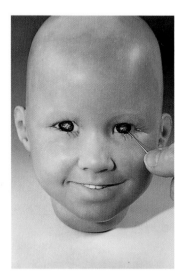

... and with a very fine needle in the still damp color, radiating lines are pulled, so as to make the iris look as natural as possible.

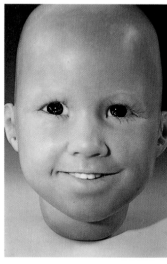

In the free space created by thinning the pupil, I paint with black Deka. After the whole eye is dried, I then varnish with colorless Deka.

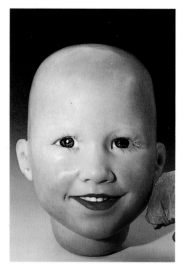

With Plaka red mixed with brown and blue, I paint the lips and gum richly and let the color soak in for a couple of hours. Absorbent paper is good for dabbing color carefully onto the cheeks.

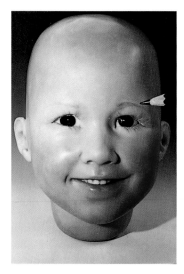
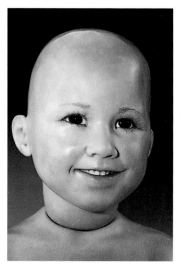
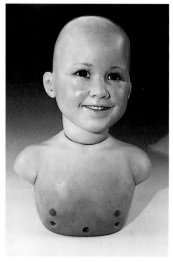

To produce lifelike lips, the color must be taken away very cautiously by dabbing with a wet brush until the mouth shimmers naturally. I varnish the teeth and the gum with colorless Deka. To be able to make corrections, I draw the eyebrows with a black colored pencil.

The final appearance of the eyebrows are then made using Plaka or Wacofin, which is painted on with a fine brush.

To stabilize the colors, the head is once more place in the oven to be fired (90°C [200°F], 60 minutes).

The connecting of head and breast plate

For the reliable connection a set-screw is affixed in the dolls neck using a polyester fast cement, which has proven to work very well.

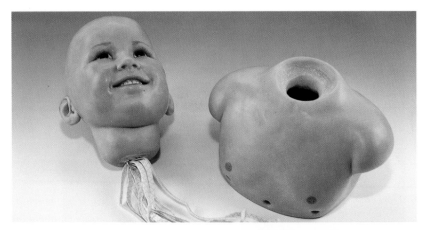

Through the ring pull 6 rubber cords and fasten the head onto the breast plate like in the illustration shown above on the right.

For each doll I choose a wig which is appropriate. With a portrait doll I try to style it, so that it looks as identical as possible to the hair style of the child, after the doll has been modelled.

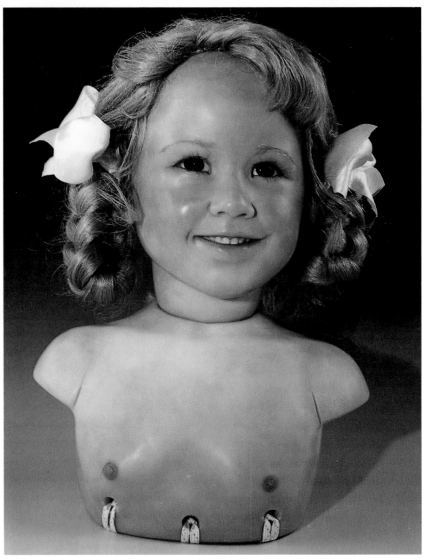

This picture shows the finished portrait breast plate doll with an individually worked wig made from undyed natural hair.

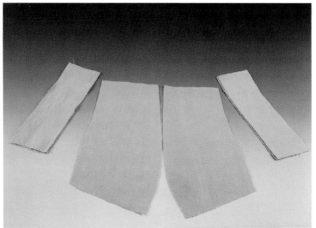

Illustration on the left: All parts of the modelling mass are now completed. The cables used as a skeleton are used on the arms for attaching them to the cloth body, while the leg cables are used not only to make these movable at the knee but also to bend them in different positions.

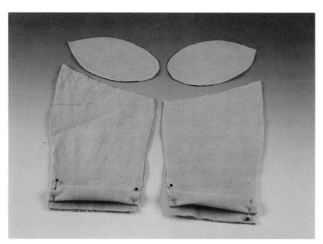

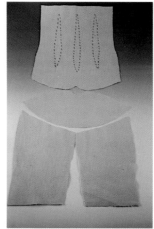

Illustrations on the right above, on the middle left and on the right: According to the patterns made by me, I cut out the individual parts of the body on the material. Rough muslin has proven to work well because of its dyeing capacity.

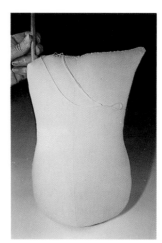

Illustration on the left and in the middle: Stitch up the parts and fill them with cotton stuffing.

Illustration on the right: Get a better fitting form for the shoulder partition on the body by turning back the pointed ends towards the inside and sewn once more together.

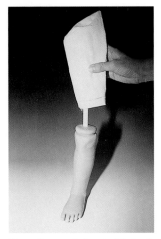

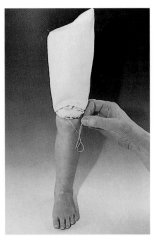

The still unstuffed part of the leg is placed over the cable, and at the groove it is firmly attached with the modelled leg. To keep the leg at the knee freely movable, a double inserted fold is anticipated (see the pattern sheets).

I have left an opening at the top so that the upper leg can now be stuffed.

It is very important that the skeleton cable remain in the middle and that it is surrounded evenly with cotton stuffing.

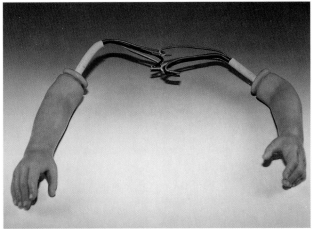

Illustration on the left: In this picture one can see the finished body, as well as the legs. Take notice that I have tied a cotton wool string in to the groove to insure a better hold.

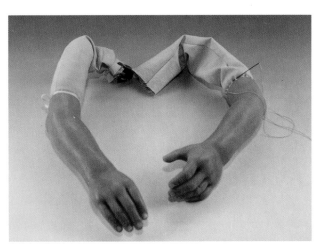

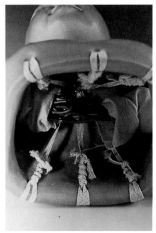

Illustration on the right above, on the left and on the right: As described with the legs, I proceed in the same way with the material portion of the arms. The material I push through the arm opening into the breast plate and connect the wiring together.

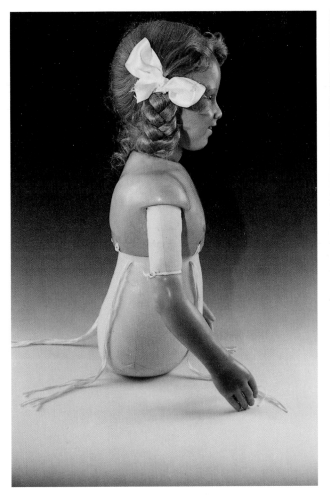

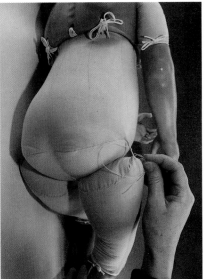

Illustration above on the left: Four long bands (approximately. 15-5/8in [40cm]) are pulled through both sides of the cloth body with a long darner. These are then fastened to the breast plate.

Elke is still naked ...

Finally I sew the legs on to the body.

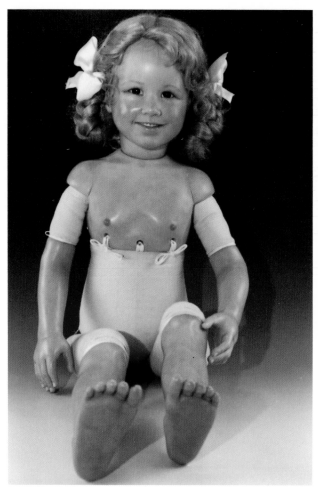

... and is slightly ashamed, ...

... she is joyfully awaiting her new beautiful clothes.

The designing and tailoring of doll clothes is a new, attractive challenge.

The doll, Elke, whose creation is described in this book, is a portrait doll. This should also be recognizable by the choice of clothing. Take the time and the trouble to knit the same pullover that the child wore at the time. I have let my imagination run free in the making of the skirt though. Ultimately I chose the material from flea market scraps of an old country cotton wool material with wonderful frills. Under it is an under skirt made from hand woven linen with old lace and roses.

Elke proudly shows herself in her new clothes.

With the clothing of the dolls I have the opportunity to become creative a second time.

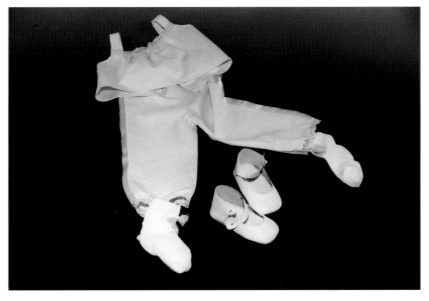

I have sewn fine linen for the underwear and embroidered them with white trims. In a children's fashion shop I found a pair of delightful socks and a pair of soft leather shoes.

Childhood photograph of Elke.

Portrait doll Elke, 33in (84cm), 1991.

*Childhood photograph
of Rotraut.*

Portrait doll Rotraut, 33in (84cm), 1990.

Childhood photograph of Irmchen.

Portrait doll Irmchen, 34-1/2in (88cm), 1985.

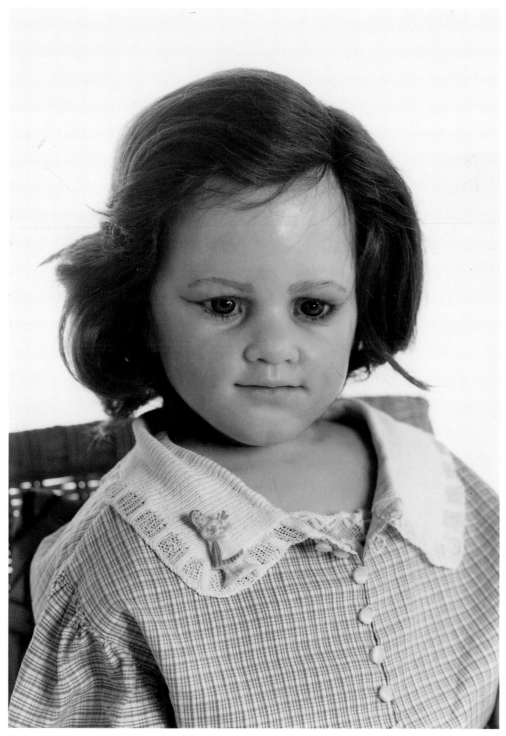

*Childhood photograph
of Sabine.*

Portrait doll Sabine, 34-1/2in (88cm), 1988.

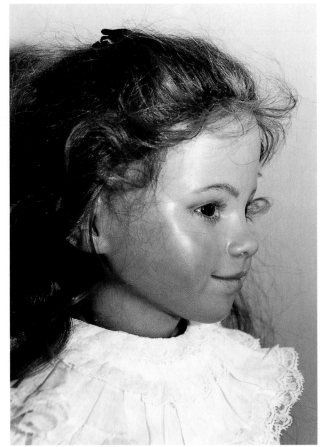

Childhood photograph of Silvia.

Portrait doll Silvia, 33in (84cm), 1991.

I fight the germ of self satisfaction through critical and positive thinking early in the first stages of creativity.

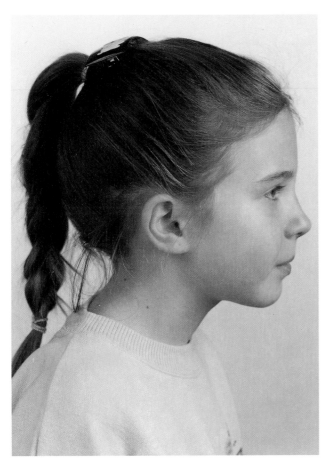

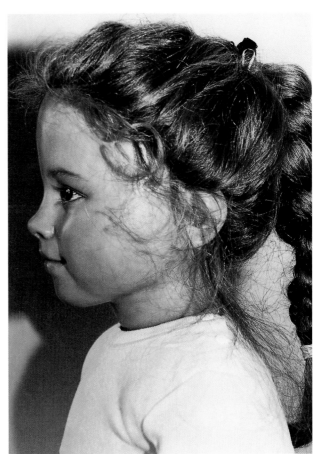

Childhood photograph of Silvia.

Portrait doll Silvia, with woven braid, 33in (84cm), 1991.

Childhood photograph of Marion.

Portrait doll Marion, 33in (84cm), 1990.

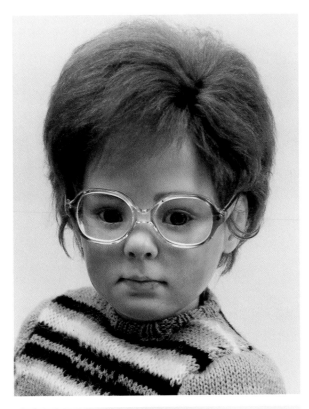

Childhood photograph of Stefan.

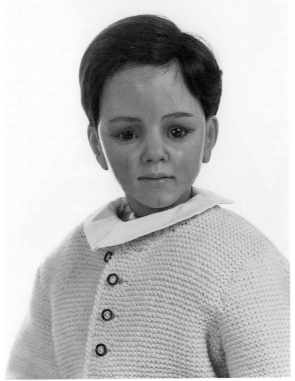

Illustration far left: Portrait doll Peterlinku, 34-1/2in (88cm), 1988.

Childhood photograph of Peterlinku.

Illustration on the right:
Childhood photograph of Christoforo.

Illustration on the left:
Childhood photograph of Marcello.

Portrait doll Christoforo, 33in (84cm), 1989.

Portrait doll Marcello, 33in (84cm), 1989.

Illustration on the right:
Childhood photograph of Christine.

Illustration on the left:
Childhood photograph of Gisela.

Illustrations on the next page:
Portrait doll Christian, 36in (91cm),
1988.
Childhood photograph of Christian.

Illustrations after the next page:
Portrait doll Nicoline, 36in (91cm),
1988.
Childhood photograph of Nicoline.

Portrait doll Christine, 33in (84cm), 1986.

Portrait doll Gisela, 33in (84cm), 1986.

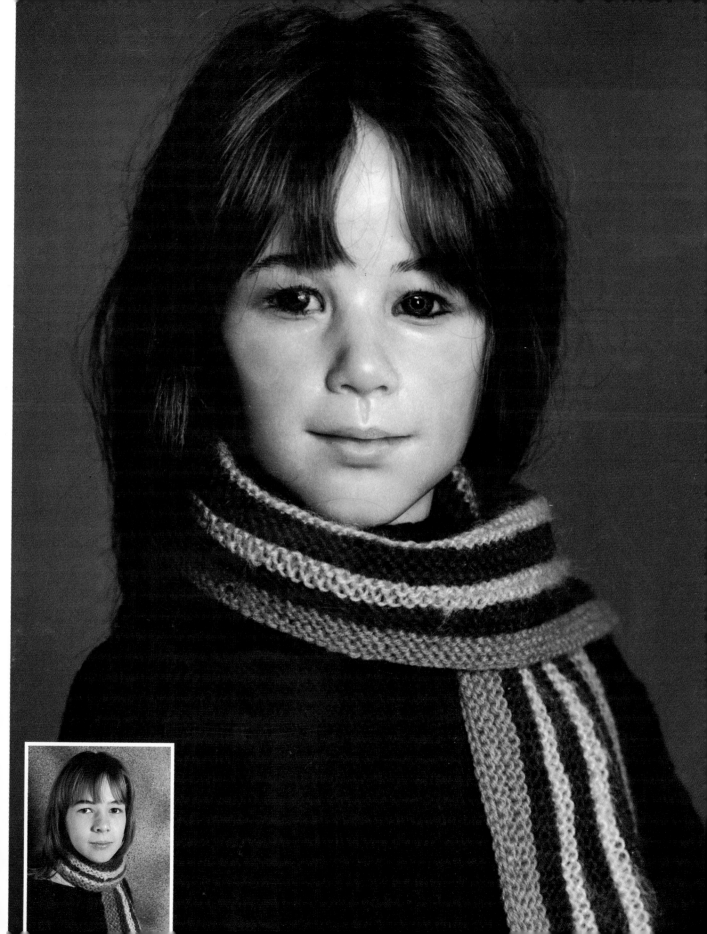

Illustration left page and above: Artist doll Ricardo, 35in (89cm), 1988.

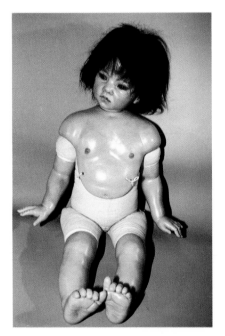

Illustration above: Artist doll PuYi without clothes.

Illustration above: Artist doll PuYi, 35in (89cm), 1988.

Illustration on the right: Artist dolls PuYi, 35in (89cm), 1988 and Suzi, 40in (100cm), 1988.

The successful work of the finished artist doll of my ideas, provides joy and an incentive for future works.

Illustration above: Artist doll Hawaiian girl, 32-1/4in (82cm), 1987.

Illustration right page: Artist doll Indian, 31in (79cm), 1985.

I direct particular attention to the proper clothing of my dolls, especially when it deals with Negroes, Indians, Asians, exotics and fairy tale doll children.

Small Japanese artist doll with molded on blossom jewels, 31-1/2in (80cm), 1983.

Fantasy and the wealth of ideas luckily have never left me sitting alone;
they are the nutrient of my success.

Illustration above and on the right: Artist doll Mitsouko, Korean, 33in (84cm), 1990.

Illustration above and on the left: Artist doll Lucia from Peru, 33in (84cm), 1991.

Only rarely does the first design of a doll fail, because usually the idea has ripened into shape in my head long before I begin to model.

*Illustration above: Artist doll, small chief with-
out headdress, 32-1/4in (82cm), 1984.*

*Illustration on the right: Artist doll standing
wearing his traditional costume.*

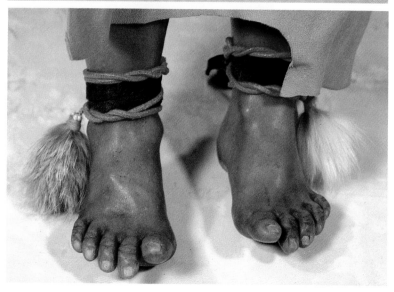

*Illustration on the right: Feet of the doll.
Illustration on the right page:
Close-up of the head.*

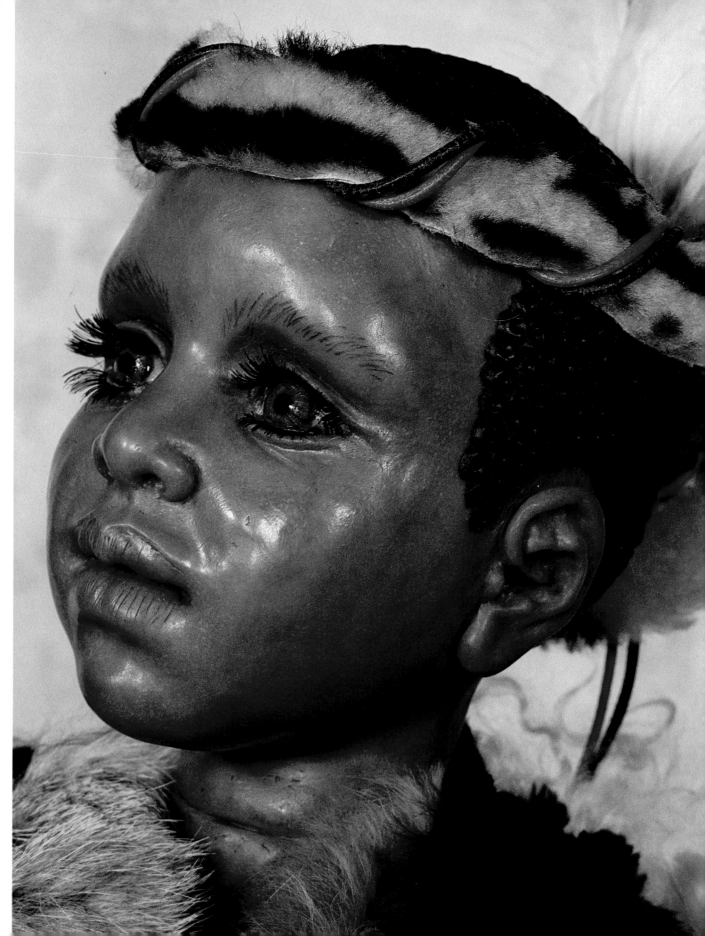

Illustration above and on the right page: Artist doll Omar, small Oriental, 33in (84cm), 1989.

It delights me to clothe my dolls creatively.

Illustration above and on the right page: Artist doll Yasmin, a ballerina, 40in (100cm), 1989.

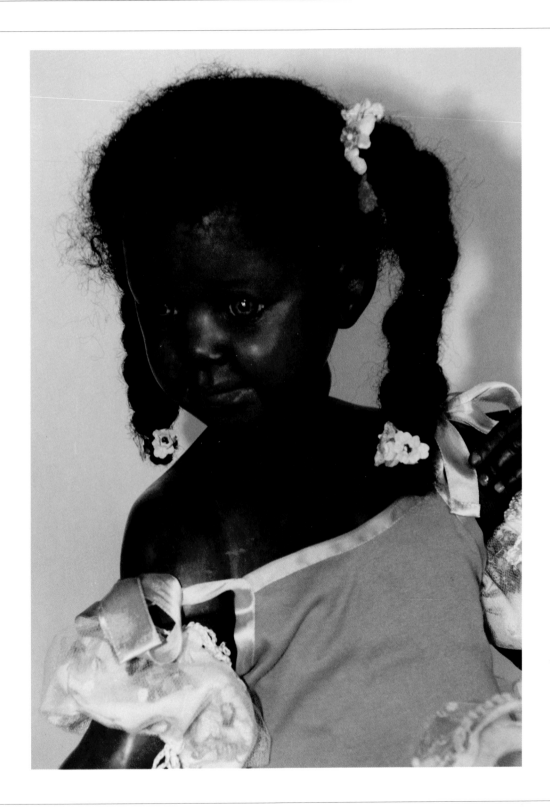

Illustration above and on the right page: Artist doll Bilan from Burkina Faso, 27-1/2in (70cm), 1991.

Illustration above and on the right page: Artist doll Red Riding Hood I, 33in (84cm), 1984.

Illustration above: Artist doll Red Riding Hood II, 33in (84cm), 1987.

Illustration on the right page: Artist dolls small Muck and the Princess, 31-1/2in (80cm) and 32-1/4in (82cm), both 1984.

At flea markets and other events I constantly look for accessories with which I can dress my original dolls.

Illustration above: Artist doll Tanja (Russian Fairy tale), 35in (89cm), 1988.
Illustration on the right page: Artist doll Cinderella, 36-1/4in (92cm), 1987.

*Illustration above and on the right page: Artist doll Katalin, Hungarian,
32in (81cm), 1989.
Illustration next page: Artist doll Mozart, 33in (84cm), 1987.
Illustration after the next page: Artist doll Eliza Doolittle, 32-1/4in (82cm), 1985.*

Illustration above and on the right page: Artist doll Manon Lescaut,
34in (86cm), 1985.

I have found my own technique which I continue to follow in
the creation of artist dolls.

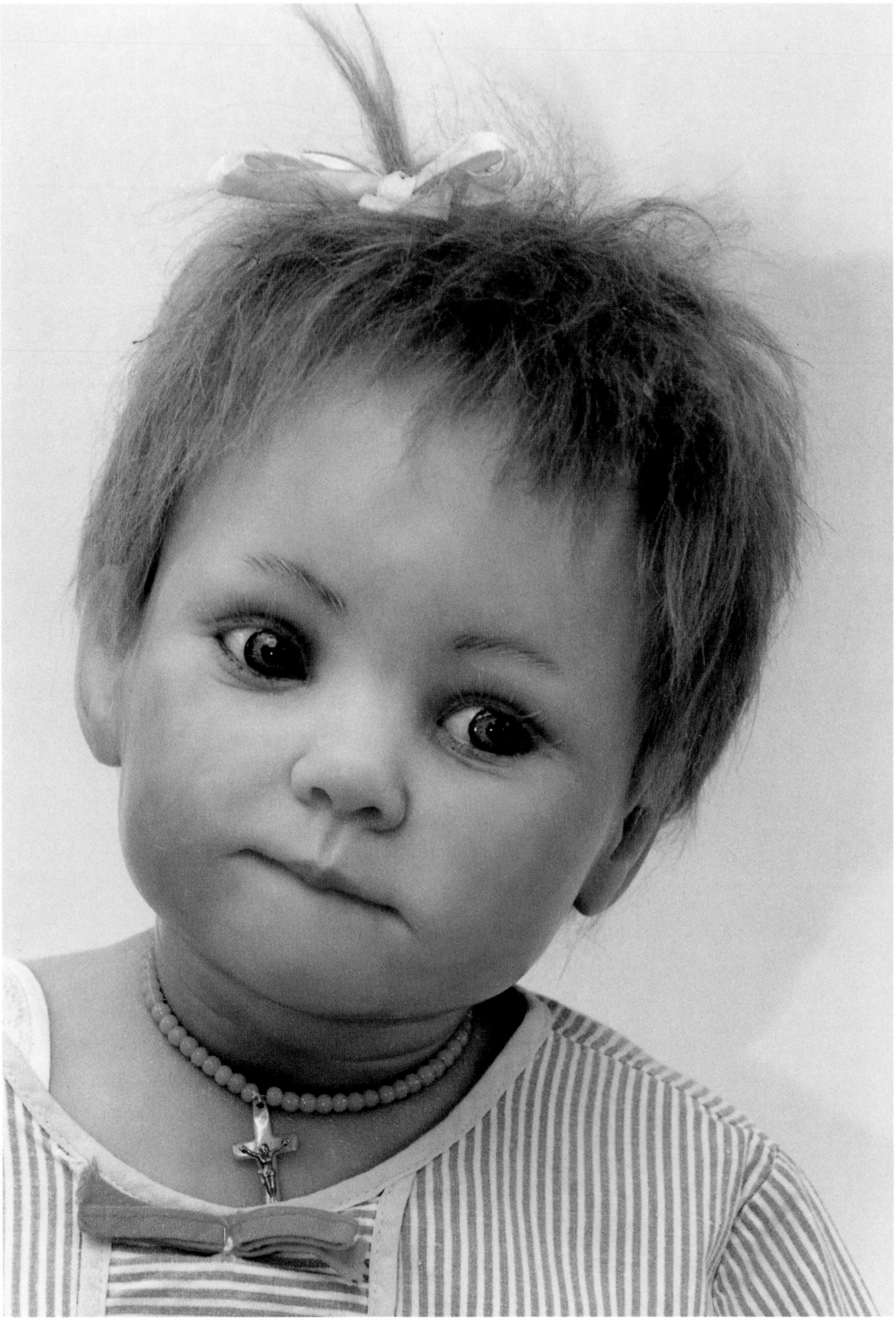

Illustration above and on the right page: Artist doll, a happy baby, 25-1/2in (65cm), 1989.

Illustration on the left: Artist doll Marlene, 40in (100cm), 1988. Illustration on the right page: Artist doll Martina, 31-1/2in (80cm), 1987.

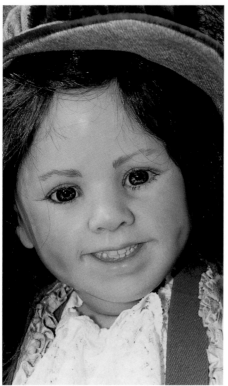

On the occasions of domestic as well as international competitions, I gladly put myself up to the criticism of a competent jury. I need this barometer.

Illustration on the far left and left: Artist doll Jennie, 33in (84cm), 1990.

Martina conquers the hearts of the American doll collectors

With the doll Martina began my close association with the Californian company "The Great American Doll Company" (GADCO).

Martina is produced in series, not only in porcelain but also in vinyl. Suzi, PuYi, Marlene, Ricardo and other brothers and sisters of the oldest and first doll, Martina, follow in the series.

The decision to release these dolls for this series has not been an easy one for me. My main concern was that Martina or Suzi, which came off the assembly line, could not be my doll anymore. This has caused hesitation. GADCO has been successful in its strivings, to come as close as possible to the original doll in the smallest details and in using the highest materials possible to produce a Rotraut-Schrott-Doll. I can then stand completely and fully behind these dolls.

In the re-creation of dolls so perfect and perceptive can only be those who place their love and whole power to the task with my dolls. For this I would like to give my particular thanks to Freddie and Michael Lam.

Illustration on the right page: Martina (Vinyl) shown
at Tiffany's in Los Angeles

Illustration above: PuYi and Suzi (vinyl), clothed lovingly and with fantasy by a collector (these clothes are not obtainable).

Illustration on the right page: Suzi and PuYi (porcelain, Gold Seal, limited edition of 250 copies), displayed at Tiffany's in Los Angeles.

Illustration on the left: Suzi and PuYi in vinyl.
Illustration below: Three small sisters of Martina in vinyl.
Illustration below on the left: Ricardo in vinyl.
Illustration below on the right: Marlene in vinyl.

Illustrations above left: Marlene in porcelain, Gold Seal, limited edition of 250 copies; above right: Marlene in porcelain, edition of 2500 copies; lower left: Yasmin and Trixie in vinyl; lower right Baby in porcelain, Gold Seal, limited edition of 250 copies.

The Artistic Heir

The dolls Suzi and PuYi, above as photograph.

Talents are bequeathed! Such is the case with Rotraut Schrott, whose father, Ludwig Adam, can rejoice because the father and daughter team now work together. Schrott creates the dolls and Adam paints these originals. If his daughter was successful in modelling life-like dolls, it is natural for him to be masterful in capturing his daughter's dolls forever on paper. One knows who Rotraut Schrott has to thank for the artistic talent. Of the first four motives of the subsequently shown dolls, the American company GADCO has produced postcards. Each dollbox contains a beautiful print of the corresponding doll.

The dolls Suzi and PuYi as watercolor.

Ricardo: Photo and watercolor.

Marlene: Photo and watercolor.

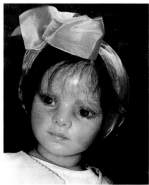

Martina: Photo and watercolor.

Katalin: Photo and watercolor.

Rotraut Schrott: Photo and water-color.

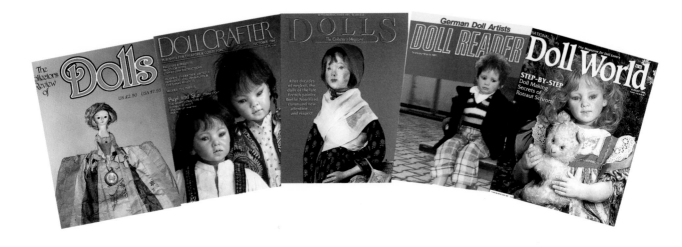

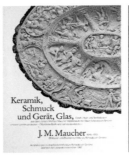

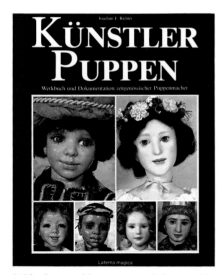

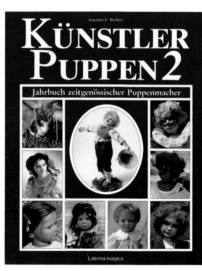

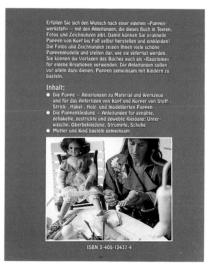

3 title photos and 9 pages text and photographic report on the artist.

7 page portfolio about Rotraut Schrott and her dolls.

Back cover and 2 page work report in the book Originelle Puppen selbstgemacht.

Postcard of the doll W. A. Mozart, published by the doll museum Stein am Rhein.

Doll, a chief's wife, for which Rotraut Schrott received in 1983 the 1st prize.

Advertising campaigns of the firm GADCO/ USA for doll series of Rotraut Schrott.

Prizes and praises have always inspired me to do still better.
                                    Rotraut Schrott

The Award of Excellence was awarded in 1988 by the Dolls magazine/USA to Rotraut Schrott for the design of the doll Martina in porcelain (on the far left).

Index